MATT CHANDLER

a beautiful design

AN UNCHANGING PLAN IN AN EVERCHANGING WORLD

Resources

LifeWay Press®
Nashville, Tennessee

Published by LifeWay Press®
© 2016 The Village Church

ISBN 9781430059806
Item 006104409

Dewey decimal classification: 234.3
Subject headings: RELIGION / CHRISTIAN MINISTRY / YOUTH

To order additional copies of this resource, write to LifeWay Church Resources Customer
Service; One LifeWay Plaza; Nashville, TN 37234-0113; fax 615.251.5933; phone toll free
800.458.2772; order online at www.lifeway.com; email orderentry@lifeway.com; or visit the
LifeWay Christian Store serving you.

Printed in the United States of America
Student Ministry Publishing
LifeWay Resources
One LifeWay Plaza
Nashville, TN 37234-0144

CONTENTS

THE AUTHOR

 MATT CHANDLER serves as the lead pastor of teaching at The Village Church in the Dallas/Fort Worth metroplex. He came to The Village in December 2002 and describes his tenure as a replanting effort to change the theological and philosophical culture of the congregation. The church has witnessed a tremendous response, growing from 160 people to more than 11,000, including campuses in Flower Mound, Dallas, Plano and Fort Worth.

Alongside his current role as lead pastor, Matt is involved in church-planting efforts both locally and internationally through The Village, as well as in various strategic partnerships. Prior to accepting the pastorate at The Village, Matt had a vibrant itinerant ministry for more than 10 years that gave him the opportunity to speak to thousands of people in America and abroad about the glory of God and the beauty of Jesus.

Matt is also the author of *The Explicit Gospel Bible Study*, *To Live Is Christ To Die Is Gain*, *The Mingling of Souls* and a coauthor of *Creature of the Word*.

Other than knowing Jesus, Matt's greatest joy is being married to Lauren and being the dad to their three children, Audrey, Reid, and Norah.

INTRODUCTION

For the vast majority of human history, there have been two culturally and socially recognized genders: women and men. Today, many leading social institutions recognize well over fifty variations of gender. There are now biological women who identify as men and biological men who identify as women. There are people who refuse to conform to any one gender and people who are currently one gender but transitioning to another. There was a time when the concept of what made someone a man or a woman was quite simple. In less than a century, culturally speaking, that has completely changed.

If there was ever a time when Christians needed to think carefully and biblically about the question of gender, that time is now.

Despite our culture's many faceted ideas and designs about gender, there is only one design that truly matters and takes precedent—God's. At the heart of the Christian faith is the belief that God created all things and that He is good. This tell us that God has a design for us, including our gender. In this study, we will seek to uncover and submit to, in Scripture, God's design for men and women.

HOW TO GET THE MOST FROM THIS STUDY

1. Attend each group experience.

- Participate in the group discussions.

2. Complete the content in this Bible study book.

- Read the introduction for each session.
- Prayerfully interact with all learning activities.
- Be honest with God, yourself, and others about your experiences.
- Apply the principles.

3. Commit to the experience.

- *A Beautiful Design* has 9 sessions with three components of personal study for each. Most groups will do this study over the course of 9 weeks, but if your group follows a different schedule, that's OK.
- Don't rush. Allow time for the Spirit of God to work in you through His Word.

IN THE
BEGINNING

WELCOME TO YOUR FIRST SESSION OF *A BEAUTIFUL DESIGN*.

Throughout this study, we will learn about God's design for men and women as those created in His image; how sin has marred that image; and how we can reconnect with His true design and purpose for our lives.

> Before we dig into our study, what are some major issues you see in the world around you?
>
> What do these issues tell us about the world in which we live?

We don't have to look very far to realize that the world in which we live is glorious. This can be seen in amazing sights like the Grand Canyon, as well as in everyday wonders like sunsets and cloudy skies. However, we don't have to look very far to realize that our world is also broken. We see this on the news through rampant crime and unexpected natural disasters. If we are honest, we see the brokenness in ourselves as we struggle to find purpose and joy in our everyday lives, too.

At the heart of the Christian faith is the belief that we serve a good God who designed us with a specific purpose and all people have failed to live according to that purpose. This week, we will focus on God's purpose for His people, and then break it down into specific applications for both guys and girls.

> What are some general ideas about the purpose of life that are prevalent among students? Specifically for young men and women?
>
> Do you think we're living in step with God's design for us? Why or why not?

SMALL GROUP STUDY

DISCUSS THE STUDY USING THE QUESTIONS BELOW.

What do you think it means to be a man? What do you think it means to be a woman?

If you asked these two questions to a random sample of students in your school or community, what kinds of answers would you likely hear?

While the answers to these questions may seem obvious to you, it is important to note that our culture answers these questions differently today than ever before. For instance, Facebook, in addition to "male" and "female," gives users 56 other ways to identify themselves with regard to gender.[1] Olympic gold medalist Bruce Jenner recently identified himself as a woman. You or your family likely know of someone who identifies as a gender other than their biological sex. Today we will see that because there is a God who created all things, including us, we are not free to define gender as we see fit. If God is truly the source and designer of all things, then we must look to Him to define us and give us purpose. Our joy and hope depend on it.

What could you or our group do to create an environment in our church and community that embraces God's design for us?

READ GENESIS 1:1.

When did God create the world?

What does the fact that God created "in the beginning" tell us about Him? What does this tell us about ourselves?

Genesis doesn't tell us the exact date God created the world. What it does say is that God created the heavens and the earth "in the beginning." This tells us something important about ourselves. We are *finite, bound by time,* we have a beginning and an end. God has neither. He exists outside of time and above time. If there is one crucial truth we must understand about God, it is this: He is not like us. He is holy. He is infinitely greater and wiser than we are.

READ 1 SAMUEL 2:2 AND ISAIAH 43:7.

In 2006, Rhonda Byrne released a book that has since sold over 19 million copies and been translated into 46 languages called, *The Secret*. In the book, Byrne claims to have found the key to a fulfilling life. She says:

> The earth turns on its orbit for You. The oceans ebb and flow for You. The birds sing for You. The sun rises and it sets for You. The stars come out for You. Every beautiful thing you see, every wondrous thing you experience, is all there for You. Take a look around. None of it can exist, without You. No matter who you thought you were, now you know the Truth of Who You Really Are. You are the master of the Universe. You are the heir to the kingdom. You are the perfection of Life. And now you know The Secret.[2]

Compare Byrne's words with 1 Samuel 2:2. What is wrong with her thinking?

If God is the source of all things, what does that tell us about our purpose in life?

Since God created us for His glory (Isa. 43:7), how should we live?

Since God is the source of all things, you are not the point. I am not the point. We are not the point of the universe. God is. He is worthy of all that we are and all that we have.

READ PROVERBS 14:12 AND PSALM 16:11.

What is promised to those who embrace God's design and submit to His plans? What is promised to those who don't?

How should knowing that God has created us and given us purpose shape the way we think about gender?

CLOSE IN PRAYER. COMPLETE PERSONAL STUDIES 1.1-1.3 BEFORE THE NEXT GROUP EXPERIENCE.

1.1
ORIGIN: WHO AM I?

The very first verse of the Bible, Genesis 1:1, answers questions that philosophers, theologians and scientists have been asking for centuries: *Who am I? Why am I here? And how do things work?*

This week's Bible study looks into each of those questions. Let's begin with the question of origin: *Who Am I?*

Read Genesis 1:1. Let's unpack this verse one phrase at a time.

IN THE BEGINNING GOD

We are finite—bound by time. But God is infinite, beyond our understanding of time. He has always been.

> Take a moment to consider the fact that God has always been. Describe your thoughts about this.

CREATED

When it comes to the account of creation, it's easy to get lost in the weeds of the hows and whens. We often have more questions than answers. The point of the Genesis account of creation is not to answer all of our questions about creation. Rather it reminds us over and over that the infinite Creator God is responsible for it all.

> Read Psalm 19:1-6. Why did God create? What does creation say about God?

> Read Colossians 1:15-17. How will you live your life differently knowing you were created *for* Him?

THE HEAVENS

Have you ever considered the size of space? Do a quick Google search and you'll find some fascinating information. If we were to travel at a velocity that pushed the human body to its limit, it would still take us millions of years to travel to the end of space. The enormity of space is absolutely mind-boggling. And our creator God simply spoke it—all of it—into existence!

> Read Psalm 147:4. Recall a time when the sky was so clear, the stars were numerous and it almost didn't seem real. Picture that moment. Now, jot down the first thought about God that comes to mind.

AND THE EARTH

In the middle of this vast universe, on a planet in one of the smaller solar systems, God placed the crown jewel of His creation—He created man and woman to glorify Him by ruling the earth. In this setting, the greatest drama in the universe would be played out. God not only created all in good order, He holds all things in place.

> What part of God's creation is the most awe-inspiring to you? Explain.

If you'll take a moment to consider the vastness of the universe, you might become a little fearful. The magnificence of creation could cause you to feel smaller than you'd like. There is Someone behind that magnificence; Someone who told that magnificence to be simply because He was able. The realization of that truth should produce an unmatched awe in our hearts.

PRAYER

Thank God for His goodness in creating a world with such immensity and beauty for our joy and His glory. Ask Him for the grace to recognize His majesty and goodness as you observe the handiwork of His creation.

1.2

PURPOSE: WHY AM I HERE?

God is the origin of all things. We know that God created the heavens and the earth in good order and for a purpose, so we can rule out all competing philosophies and belief systems. A few are listed below. Under each one, explain why you believe it cannot be true. (*Hint: Look back to Genesis 1:1.*)

Dualism: Good and evil are two competing forces in which the victor is unclear.

Materialism: The idea that all that exists is the physical world. This is not the same as capitalistic materialism, or considering possessions as highly important.

Polytheism: The belief in more than one god.

Hedonism: The belief that the pursuit of pleasure should be our ultimate purpose.

Existentialism: Man wills and determines his own reality.

Pantheism: The belief that all of nature is one with God.

Since God is the origin of all things, then by default, only He can determine the purpose for all things. Nothing in the cosmos—you and I included—floats aimlessly through time. We have a creator who made us with a purpose in mind. As created beings, we must look to God to find purpose and meaning for our lives.

Do you live each day like you were created with a purpose? If yes, jot down an example below. If no, why not?

If someone were to ask you, "What is God's purpose for your life?" What would you say?

In Romans 1, the apostle Paul gave a clear description of the wrong choices we can make when we look for value, meaning and purpose in things other than our Creator.

Read Romans 1:18-25. Then, summarize these verses, paying special attention to verse 25.

Note one area where you consistently look to the world (created things) for purpose or meaning. What would change in your life if you began to look to God and His good design instead?

Read Ephesians 2:10. What word did Paul use to describe people? Why is this important?

PRAYER

As you conclude your study today, thank God for creating you with purpose. Ask God to help you clearly see the good works He created you for.

1.3

MAN'S PURPOSE

There is a way we have been designed to work. There is a good, right and beautiful design implemented by the Creator of all things.

Read Proverbs 14:12. Summarize the verse in your own words.

This is a terrifying verse. We will face a multitude of decisions and situations that push us to decide what is the right thing to do or the right way to go. And sometimes, what seems to us to be the right way is actually the road to destruction. This is especially true when we try to forge our own way in life.

Can you think of a time when you thought you were going the "right" way, but you ended up in a bad spot? Describe your experience.

There is a difference between existing and living. Just because you're breathing air doesn't mean you're truly living. What the Bible says in Proverbs 14:12, is that God, the Creator of everything, makes known to us the path of life. He says to us, "Do you want to know what manhood is? Here's the path of life. Do you want to know what womanhood is? Here's the path of life. You want to know about money? Here's the path of life. Sex? Here's the path of life. Children? Here's the path of life."

In your everyday life, do you tend to see God's path as leading to life or leading to constraint? Explain.

In John 10:10 Jesus used similar language. The answers to the following questions are obvious, but let's write it out in black and white so we can really grasp the paradox here.

What does the thief come to do?

And why has Jesus come?

Being the object of someone's stealing, killing and destroying is not at the top of most of our bucket lists. Life. That's what we want. And we want the best one possible.

Are you living outside of God's purpose for your life? Are you allowing the thief to steal your joy, peace and security? Are you walking your own path to life instead of following the Lord's? If so, confess this to Him. Repent and receive His grace, turning your life to walk again in His way. In so doing, may your life proclaim to our broken, sin-scarred world that God's way is best.

How would you explain the difference between God's good design for the world and its present condition?

Why do you think the world has deviated from God's good design?

PRAYER

Conclude this week's Bible study by praying Psalm 16:11. Ask God to make known to you His good design and how you can live it out in a way that leads to flourishing for you and the people around you.

IN HIS IMAGE

WELCOME TO SESSION 2 OF *A BEAUTIFUL DESIGN*.

Take a few minutes to review what we discussed in the previous session.

READ GENESIS 1:1 AND PSALM 16:11.

How did last week's session challenge your thinking about your purpose in life?

Are you sometimes tempted to think that submitting to God's design of the world holds you back or keeps you from doing the things you want?

In *Mere Christianity*, C. S. Lewis talked about "the machine" or how things work:

> There is a story about a schoolboy who was asked what he thought God was like. He replied that, as far as he could make out, God was "The sort of person who is always snooping around to see if anyone is enjoying himself and then trying to stop it." And I am afraid that is the sort of idea that the word "Morality" raises in a good many people's minds: something that interferes, something that stops you having a good time. In reality, moral rules are directions for running the human machine. Every moral rule is there to prevent a breakdown, or a strain, or a friction, in the running of that machine. That is why these rules at first seem to be constantly interfering with our natural inclinations. When you are being taught how to use any machine, the instructor keeps on saying, "No, don't do it like that," because, of course, there are all sorts of things that look all right and seem to you the natural way of treating the machine, but do not really work.[1]

How do you tend to view rules? What about God's commands? What steps could you take to view them as they're intended?

Look at Psalm 16:11. How can you be more mindful of God's good design for life? How does submitting to His good design bring joy?

SMALL GROUP STUDY

DISCUSS THE STUDY USING THE QUESTIONS BELOW.

Ask the girls in your group, what makes women unique from men? Ask the boys in your group, what makes men unique from women?

In what ways are women and men the same?

We could talk all day about the differences we perceive between women and men, but the reality is that they are far more alike than they are different. At the heart of what men and women share in common is what theologians refer to as the *imago Dei*. Today, we will consider what it means to be made in the image of God and how that relates to the way we think about and interact with the people around us.

READ GENESIS 1:24-31.

How are people similar to everything else God made? How are they different?

What does it mean to be made "in the image of God"? What unique tasks has God given men and women?

Rulers in the Ancient Near East built statues and placed icons all over the various lands they ruled to signify that those lands fell under their rule. As men and women made in God's image, you and I are the icons of His rule on earth. As God's image bearers, we were created to reflect His reign and rule over the world. Through us, as His image bearers on earth, God reveals Himself as the reigning and ruling Creator. This is God's investment in humanity—God-like glory, along with moral capacity to reign and rule the earth as His representatives. This is what sets us apart from the rest of creation.

What unique tasks did God give to His image bearers? What does this tell you about your purpose in life?

When God created man and woman in His image, He told them to fill the earth and subdue it—they were to spread out and utilize the world's resources to help them thrive. Twice we read that God gave them *dominion*, or *authority*, over the created order. Though God is the source and ultimate ruler over all, God gave us dominion, meaning He put us in charge of the world He created. We are to exercise authority and bring order to the chaos. This is something that animals cannot do. They are not made in the image of God and, as a result, are chaotic.

God not only created a good world for Adam and Eve, but also gave them the privilege of ruling over it. This was a tremendous act of love and it should remind us that our ultimate purpose in life is to glorify God. We should exercise good dominion—we should take such good care of the world that we point people to God's perfect goodness and authority over all things.

> How should knowing that all people were made in the image of God change the way we think about and interact with others?

> What evidence do you see that people in our culture do not recognize the image of God in one another (racism, pornography, celebrity culture, etc.)?

The implication of the *imago Dei* is that there is intrinsic human dignity that places us above everything else in the created order. All people have *intrinsic value*, meaning *they have value that naturally belongs to them*. Our culture's greatest sins are all rooted in a failure to understand and apply the *imago Dei*. Pornography denies the image of God in others by turning them into objects for our sexual pleasure. When we discriminate, we make assumptions about others based on their race or social status, thereby denying the image of God in them.

> After creating mankind, God says His creation is "very good." What is the significance of that phrase? How does it relate to the *imago Dei*?

> How should knowing that we were made in the image of God change the way we see ourselves?

Knowing that you were made in the image of God gives you worth, value and dignity that no one can take away from you. Guys—don't measure yourself by your success or lack of success in relationships with girls. Girls—don't measure your worth by the way guys see you. You are valuable to God. Period. When we see others primarily as image bearers, as representatives of God, we will honor them. Guys will treat girls as sisters and girls will treat guys as brothers.

CLOSE IN PRAYER. COMPLETE PERSONAL STUDIES 2.1-2.3 BEFORE THE NEXT GROUP EXPERIENCE.

2.1
WHAT IS IMAGO DEI?

After God created the heavens and the earth, all the unique wildlife, fruit trees and sandy beaches, He created man and woman. Genesis 1:26 tells us that the Godhead created man in their image. For centuries, theologians have referred to this doctrine as the *imago Dei*.

Through *imago Dei*, God invested in humanity—His creation to whom He gave authority to rule over all other creation.

Though the phrase *image of God* only appears twice in the Old Testament (Genesis 1:26-27; 5:1-3), its importance to a proper theological understanding of the condition of humanity cannot be overstated.

Essentially, a proper understanding of *imago Dei* gives direction to every part of your day.

> In this week's group session, we unpacked Genesis 1:26-28. In light of this passage, what are some ways we are called to reflect (image) God in the world?

> How often does knowing you are a reflection of God influence your decision making?

> List two changes you intend to make this week to more clearly reflect the image of God.

Read Psalm 139:13-16. Summarize each verse in your own words.

Verse 13:

Verse 14:

Verse 15:

Verse 16:

These verses indicate that God's image is not placed in us at birth. Rather, God created the blueprint for us before we were conceived, and then constructed us in His image to those exact specs.

> In *The Weight of Glory*, C. S. Lewis wrote, "There are no ordinary people. You have never talked to a mere mortal. It is immortals whom we joke with, work with, marry, snub, and exploit."[2] Which people in your life have you had a difficult time interacting with? How might your interactions with them change if you made an effort to acknowledge the image of God in them?

If every person is created in the image of God, then every person has infinite value. That God creates and ordains the days of each human life gives significance and infinite value to each life.[3] This has major implications when it comes to some of the worst atrocities of our day.

PRAYER

The image of God describes not just something we have, but something we are. Conclude your study today by asking the Lord to break through the lies we have believed about ourselves and others and refocus our eyes on being God's image bearers. Ask Him to give you the grace to see everyone you engage with just as they are—infinitely valuable.

2.2
IMPLICATIONS

It only takes a quick scroll through social media to be reminded that we, as humans, have marred the image of God. All over the Internet we see disturbing videos from abortion clinics. And news stories tell us that human trafficking is a growing problem, even here in the United States. Something is not right. If we are made in the image of God, no matter our age, race, status or circumstances, we have value. But often we are treated and treat others contrary to that truth. Let's look at some issues that illustrate how we distort the image of God in ourselves and others.

ABORTION

Read Psalm 139:16. When does God write our days into His book? What does this tell us about God? About ourselves?

We should be amazed by God's detailed design of life. The text of Psalm 139 emphasizes that He is building us in our mother's womb for the things He has planned for us—God deeply values all human life and so should we.

With what we know from Scripture and science, how should we view abortion? How does abortion tear at the heart of the *imago Dei*?

SLAVERY AND HUMAN TRAFFICKING

According to the International Labor Organization, there are an estimated 5.5 million child victims of trafficking in the world. This is not just a problem in other countries, human trafficking has been reported in all 50 states as well.[4]

How do slavery and human trafficking demean human life? How does the knowledge of this practice affect you?

RACIAL PREJUDICE AND INJUSTICE

In Luke 10:25-37, we read the familiar story of the good Samaritan. Jesus told this parable knowing that most Jews held a very prejudicial view of Samaritans.

> Read Luke 10:25-37. What did Jesus tell the expert in the law he had to do to inherit eternal life? What question did the expert ask in response?

The law expert was hoping to be able to rule out loving certain people in his life and world. Instead, Jesus told a story that rocked his world. Even as we read the story today, we wonder why the priest didn't stop to help. Ministry is his job! We expect the Levite, who would have been an assistant to the priests, would render aid to the injured man. Instead, it was the Samaritan, whose race was seen as inferior and without value. Through this story, Jesus is clear about who our neighbors are (everyone), as well as how we are to view and relate to them. Jesus calls us to love and serve our neighbors self-sacrificially.

SEXUAL SIN

Prostitution, strip clubs and pornography. All are a part of the disgraceful distortion we have made of God's plan for sex.

> Read 1 Corinthians 6:12-20. How does sexual immorality dishonor the Lord? How does it dishonor our neighbors made in His image? How can we guard against it?

PRAYER

Maybe you haven't personally struggled in these areas, but you have remained silent while these issues plague our society. It's time to stand up. Pray for God's direction in how you can join the fight.

2.3
THE IMAGO DEI IN MY LIFE

Men and women are different. It's no secret.

Men tend to be physically stronger than women. They are generally realistic, objective and logical. Oppositely, women are usually idealistic, subjective and emotional. Now, this is all generally speaking. There are always exceptions. Neither one's traits are superior to the other's. Both have their strengths. Both have their weaknesses.

Just like there is no higher race, there is also no higher gender. God had a purpose in making each gender to function a certain way. He made us different, and the same. We bear His image.

> Because men and women are created in the image of God, they share many characteristics and gifts. What are some of the attributes men and women share?

> How do these character traits differ from how students in your school view men and women? Why do you think it is important for us to identify and celebrate the ways men and women are united as image bearers?

The fact that men and women are both created in the image of God should define the way we view each other. Because of the *imago Dei*, the stereotypes of men being childish and women being no more than pretty faces must cease.

> Think of a time you saw our culture's stereotypical views on masculinity and femininity play out. Maybe it was a movie, commercial or a conversation with a friend. Did you agree with that view or feel threatened by it? What kind of feelings did it stir up in you?

Galatians 3:26-29 tells us that no matter our race or gender, if we have placed our faith in Jesus, we are one in Him. This reminds us that we must put away all false ideas of superiority and inferiority. God made us equal. He gave both sexes intellect, passions and gifts. As sons and daughters of God, we are expected to fulfill His purpose. We should support one another as we do this together, and treat one another as brothers and sisters, not objects to be consumed.

For Guys: Have you ever been tempted to treat girls as objects for your pleasure? Explain. Why is it easy to fall into this practice?

For Girls: Have you ever been tempted to stereotype guys? Explain. Why is it easy to fall into this practice?

Jot down some ways you can stop the drift toward stereotypes and value the opposite gender as God's image-bearers. How can you celebrate the similarities and differences between the genders?

PRAYER

Thank God for creating us in His image. Thank Him for the glorious truth that men and women share a common identity and purpose before the Lord.

MAN'S PURPOSE

WELCOME TO YOUR GROUP EXPERIENCE FOR SESSION 3 OF *A BEAUTIFUL DESIGN*.

Take a few minutes to review what we discussed in the previous session.

> What does it mean to be made in the image of God?

> Has the way you view the people around you changed since last week's study? How so?

> How can we fight the temptation to use and belittle other people?

All people, male and female, were made in the image of God; therefore we are equal in importance and worth. When we fail to understand that people are made in the image of God, there will be all sorts of temptations to consume, use, belittle and rob them of dignity. The world's greatest human injustices—racism, poverty, sexism, discrimination and pornography—can all be traced to a failure to understand and recognize the *imago Dei*.

> How can we grow to have more empathy for those who are different from us?

Followers of Christ should have a higher view of people than anyone else. Knowing that all people are created in God's image tells us that all people have value. Their stories, concerns and experiences deserve to be heard. If we hope to grow in Christ, we must grow in our love for one another. Such growth requires being quick to hear and slow to speak (Jas. 1:19).

SMALL GROUP STUDY

DISCUSS THE STUDY USING THE QUESTIONS BELOW.

What is your dream job? Why?

What is the worst job you have ever had? Why?

Today's study is the first of three sessions exploring how God designed men. When men fulfill the purpose and design of men as the Bible outlined it, humanity flourishes. When men refuse to step into the space they are called to fill, conflict and strife reign. Today, we will look specifically at how God has designed men to work and to lead.

READ GENESIS 2:1-17.

For what purpose did God place man in the Garden (vv. 15-17)? What does this tell us about Him?

Was Eve present when God commanded Adam to work and keep the Garden? What does this tell us about God's design for men?

God placed Adam in the Garden prior to creating Eve for the purpose of working and keeping it. Here we see the principle of male headship (1 Cor. 11:3; Eph. 5:22-33; Col. 3:18). This does not mean that men are, in any way, superior to women. *Headship* is *the unique leadership of the man in the work of establishing order for human flourishing.* We see God's goodness in His design for men when He graciously provided the Garden as a home for Adam and entrusted to him the sacred task of protecting and caring for it. Though God is King over all creation, He willingly shared His creation with man and gave him dominion over it (Gen. 1:26-28). When we go to work, we are living out God's design.

If men image God by working, what do they communicate when they are lazy or refuse to work (Prov. 6:6-11; 1 Tim. 5:8)?

The fact that God commanded Adam to work the Garden prior to sin's entrance, tells us something important about work—it is good. One of the ways God designed men to glorify Him is by working hard and providing for their families. When men are lazy and refuse to work, they are not the only ones who suffer—their spouses, families and friends suffer as well. When men shrink back from God's good design, society itself suffers as a result. As students, the vast majority of you are not in a place where you can work a full-time job, but that doesn't mean that you should not begin living out this aspect of God's design. You can reflect the image of God by studying hard, joyfully helping with projects around your house and looking for opportunities to learn valuable life skills.

READ EPHESIANS 5:25-31.

> How did Paul instruct men to love their wives (v. 25)? How does this differ from our culture's understanding of love?

> What is the goal of a man loving his wife self-sacrificially?

> What are the implications for single young men? Explain.

Paul's command to men presents us with a radically different definition of love than that of our culture. Our culture defines love primarily as a feeling, but Paul said the love a man should have for his wife is primarily about commitment, spiritual leadership and self-sacrifice. Paul challenged men to love their wives in such a way that they point them to Christ and encourage spiritual growth in them. Therefore, single young men should fight against the temptation to rush into relationships with young women and instead seek to cultivate godly character. Similarly, young women should raise the bar for young men by setting higher expectations for them.

CLOSE IN PRAYER. COMPLETE PERSONAL STUDIES 3.1-3.3 BEFORE THE NEXT GROUP EXPERIENCE.

3.1

THE MASCULINE HEART

What if you were to ask 100 people the simple question, "What does it mean to be a man?" One would be hard-pressed to find a time throughout human history in which the answers would be more diverse than they are today. For our definition, we must not consult public opinion or even the opinion of expert psychologists. As helpful as that might be, what matters most is what the Word of God has to say.

Read Genesis 2:15. What was the job God gave Adam to do?

Before sin marred the completeness of God's image in Adam, God gave him the responsibility of working and keeping the Garden. God beautifully designed an environment for Adam to have a joyful, fulfilling life. Like Adam, God has placed every man on the planet in a "garden" in which he has the opportunity to work for the good of the world or create chaos.

For Men: Are you working for the good of the world or merely creating chaos? How can you tell?

For Women: Recognize the weighty responsibility that is placed on the men in your life. Pray that God would strengthen them for the task at hand.

The task that God has called men to is tough. It is not for the faint of heart. But the good news is that God has hard-wired the masculine heart with the tools needed to accomplish this task.

Read Genesis 2:15-16. Record in your own words the command God gave to Adam.

Notice that before God created Eve, He first gave to Adam a framework of His beautiful design for men. Why do you think this is?

If any marriage, church or society is to succeed and prosper it needs men willing to pour out their lives out for the sake others. We need men to act like men by submitting to God's commands in response to His beautiful design.

PRAYER

Girls, pray for the men in your life. Many men are weary. The weight and responsibility of the call to serve and sacrificially love can become overwhelming. Pray that men will embrace this call with joy and confidence and recognize they cannot fulfill the responsibility given to them without the power of the Holy Spirit. Pray that God would give them grace to live in the fullness of this call.

If you are a young man, pray that God would be working in you now to prepare to one day be a godly father and husband should you chose to marry and start a family. Pray that God would instill in you a desire to love, lead and serve others self-sacrificially.

3.2

A UNIQUE RESPONSIBILITY

Where single men treat women like sisters in Christ recognizing the *imago Dei* in them, co-ed interaction flourishes. Where men tune in and lead spiritually in the home and in the church, those homes and churches flourish.

Headship is *the unique leadership of the man in the work of establishing order for human flourishing.*

Where men refuse to step into the space they are called to fill, the world suffers. This is true economically, sociologically and spiritually. What happens when men refuse to be husbands and fathers? Things break. Statistics prove it.[1]

Most, if not all of us, have witnessed first-hand the direct results of men shirking their responsibility. (More on this next week.) However, we have probably also seen the positive results of a husband/father leading his family. Men carry a tremendous amount of influence.

> Read Acts 16:25-27. What was the jailer's reaction to finding the prisoners unchained?

Rather than seeing this as an opportunity for escape, Paul and Silas saw the jailer's brokenness as an opportunity to minister to him.

> Read Acts 16:28-30. How did the jailer respond to Paul's announcement that all prisoners were accounted for?

> Before you go further with your study, stop and thank God for your own salvation.

Now read verses 31-34. What happened in the jailer's family as a result of his new relationship with Christ?

This incredible story illustrates a powerful biblical truth: Typically, it is the man who sets the spiritual climate in the home. In homes where men embrace the responsibility to be the spiritual leaders, Scripture, prayer and the reality of God becomes the climate of the home. It is in this climate where the lives of wives and children flourish.

Kids follow daddy. It has been said by many well-meaning youth or children's pastors, "If you reach the children, you will reach the family." While this sounds good, it's just not true. In fact, when a child comes to faith in Christ, the family will only follow suit 3.5% of the time. The probability of the family following when mom is reached first is a little better at 17%. But when dad comes to faith in Christ the rest of the family follows 93% of the time.[2]

While these realities may seem irrelevant to you at your current stage of life as a student, the opposite is actually the case. As young men and women, it is imperative that you recognize God's design for men so that you can begin actively encouraging and supporting the men in your life—your father, grandfather, brothers, pastors and friends.

PRAYER

Thank God for the men in your life and pray for Him to strengthen them as they become the leaders He always intended them to be. Guys, even now, you can pray that God would prepare your heart to serve Him according to His design within a family and in life.

3.3
JESUS IS THE MODEL

List the qualities that best describe your traditional understanding
of Jesus?

To find the best example of what God intended man to be, we look no further
than the God-man Himself—Jesus Christ. However, when most of us think
about manhood, Jesus is not the first man that comes to mind. In fact, many
people see Jesus as a tender, feather-haired, blue-eyed wimp of a man. When
perceived this way, it's difficult for men to identify with Him.

This false perception of Jesus can result in a wrong understanding of Christian
manhood. Charles H. Spurgeon once said, "There has got abroad a notion,
somehow, that if you become a Christian (or little Christ) you must sink
your manliness and turn milksop [weak and indecisive]." That makes a true
understanding of Jesus imperative for men.

Let's take a look at a few verses that will help give a us a clear picture of Jesus.

Read the following verses, what does each tell you about Jesus, the
perfect man?

John 8:1-11

Matthew 23:27

Matthew 17:17

Mark 11:15-17

Revelation 19:11-21

John 13:1-15

Matthew 11:29

Which of these characteristics do you image most effectively? In what ways?

Which characteristics do you struggle with the most? In what way?

What steps can you take to strengthen these areas in your life?

Eric Mason, in his book *Manhood Restored* said, "Men are only as manly as it relates to the standard set by Jesus."[3] If men are going to live in the fullness of biblical manhood, they must model themselves after Jesus, the prototype man who was tempted in every way yet without sin (Heb. 4:15). The reality is that every man will walk in the shadow of one of two men: Adam or Jesus.

Romans 5:18-19 provides a stark contrast of the first Adam and the second Adam, Jesus. Which contrasting statement stands out most to you and why?

PRAYER

As you conclude this week's personal Bible study, commit to walk in the shadow of Jesus, the new Adam, the man who was man enough to drink in death and spit out victory. Read Romans 5:20. The apostle Paul gives us a poignant picture of God's grace, "where sin increased, grace abounded all the more." Take a few minutes to repent from areas of life where you are walking in the shadow of the first Adam. Thank God for His grace and commit to walk in the fullness of Christ.

MAN'S HURDLES

WELCOME TO YOUR GROUP EXPERIENCE FOR SESSION 4 OF *A BEAUTIFUL DESIGN*.

Take a few minutes to review what we discussed in the previous session.

In what ways did God uniquely design men?

Why is it important that we, as students, think carefully about God's design for men and women?

If you are a young man, how are you striving to live out God's design for manhood?

If you are a young woman, how can you support the young men in our group throughout that process?

Last week we discussed how men are meant to lead their wives through loving, serving and protecting. While most of you are not yet married, it is important to have a vision for the kind of man or woman you want to be. Without such a vision, you will be passive and conform to our culture's warped understanding of manhood and womanhood. Today we will discuss the selfish nature of passivity and how we might catch an active, humble, giving and Christ-like vision for manhood.

SMALL GROUP STUDY

DISCUSS THE STUDY USING THE QUESTIONS BELOW.

> Aside from the obvious physical differences, what distinguishes men from boys? What distinguishes women from girls?

Research suggests that young people are taking longer to grow up than ever before. Twenty-somethings are waiting longer to do things that have traditionally been identified with adulthood, things like buying a home, getting married, starting a career and having children.[1] It is important to note that getting married and having children do not turn a boy into a man. Scripture defines this transition differently. As we discovered last week, the primary indicator that a boy has turned into a man is loving, self-sacrificial leadership (Gen. 2:24; Eph. 5:25). By that definition, it would seem that there are far more boys in our culture than men. Today, we will discuss why that is—the biggest barriers to seeing and embracing God's design for manhood.

READ GENESIS 3:1-5.

> Who is the serpent? How else is he described in the Bible (John 8:44; 2 Cor. 4:4; Eph. 2:2; 1 Pt. 5:8; Rev. 12:9)? How did he tempt Adam and Eve?

> Why do you think so many people in our culture reject God's design for women and men?

Satan, the great deceiver, sought to get Adam and Eve to question God's design for the world. He got Adam and Eve thinking that God was somehow holding out on them by telling them not to eat of one tree in the Garden. Part of the reason so many people today reject God's design for manhood is because they think it is oppressive. They fear they will miss out on something. As we progress through Genesis, we will see that nothing could be further from the truth—submitting to God's design leads to lasting joy.

READ GENESIS 3:6-13.

> What was Adam doing while Eve was being tempted? What does this tell us about him?

> What was the root of Adam and Eve's sin? Explain.

At the heart of Adam and Eve's sin was pride. They gave into the lie that God was holding out on them, questioned His authority and expressed a desire to stand in His place as Lord of their own lives. Adam passively stood by while his wife was tempted. Such passivity is selfish—Adam was so focused on himself that he missed a crucial opportunity exercise His God given manhood by loving, serving and protecting his wife.

> How did sin affect Adam and Eve's relationship? Their view of themselves?

> With sin's entrance into the world, the harmony of God's perfect creation was broken. How does sin affect our relationship with God and with others?

Prior to eating of the Tree of the Knowledge of Good and Evil, Adam and Eve were naked and unashamed and they walked freely in the garden with God. After eating, they were suspicious of one another and terrified of God. Their sin resulted in a loss of identity and purpose, corrupting the image of God in them.

READ GENESIS 3:14-24.

> How would sin hinder Adam from living out God's design for men (vv. 15,17-19)? How do you see this playing out today?

> What has God promised to do about the serpent (v. 15)? How can manhood be restored to God's good design?

Thanks to his decision to sin, instead of being joyful and fulfilling, Adam's work would be difficult. Instead of respecting, honoring and delighting in his wife, because of sin, Adam would be tempted to arrogantly rule over and abuse his wife. Through the curses of the fall listed in these verses, we see that sin has forever changed our understanding of and ability to live out God's design. However, there is good news hidden in these curses. God would one day destroy the serpent through the woman's offspring (v. 15). By dying on the cross Jesus rendered Satan powerless over all who believe in Him and offers to redeem us, every part of us, including our vision of manhood.

CLOSE IN PRAYER. COMPLETE PERSONAL STUDIES 4.1-4.3 BEFORE THE NEXT GROUP EXPERIENCE.

4.1

MARRED MANHOOD

Paradise on earth. The Garden of Eden was the perfect home for Adam and his wife. They had vegetation that was beautiful to look at and tasty to eat. They lived without guilt or shame. Not only was there a beautiful sense of security with each other, but also God walked among them in complete intimacy in the Garden. They had everything they needed. God told Adam that they could eat of any tree in the Garden but one. And that's the one the enemy used to tempt Eve.

Read Genesis 2:9. Name the two trees were in the midst of the Garden.

In verse 17, to whom did God give the command about not eating from the forbidden tree? Why is this significant?

What did God say would happen if they ate of the Tree of the Knowledge of Good and Evil?

Read Genesis 3:1-3. What did Eve tell the snake would be the result of eating of this tree?

It is interesting to note that God gave Adam the command about the forbidden tree and with that command came the responsibility of ensuring the safety of his wife. It seems from Scripture that Eve was not in the picture when the command was given. So it would have been Adam's responsibility to pass the instructions along.

Regardless of whether Adam relayed the instructions accurately or if Eve didn't pay attention to God's command, she acted in disobedience when she took the fruit and ate it. However, we need to note that Scripture makes it clear that Adam was with her when this all went down. They acted out of selfishness and failed to ask God for help. They became their own gods and the flourishing of creation was marred.

THE EFFECTS

Let's move from Genesis to Romans. Read Romans 5:12 and fill in the blanks:

_____ entered the world through _____ man. That man was _____. Because of sin, _____ spread to all men.

Adam lived to be 930 years old, so we know eating the forbidden fruit did not cause immediate death. However, he was banished from the Garden where God provided everything he needed to a desert where he would endure hard physical labor until he died. Sin took it's toll on Adam and Eve, introducing physical and spiritual death. Since that time, sin has devastated and marred everything, manhood included.

Because of the Fall, relationship, service and protection are now replaced with things like sexism, violence and passivity. Insecurity characterizes generation after generation of men in a continually increasing way. Even the most godly display of manhood is only a faint echo of what God designed men to be.

PRAYER

Men: Pray that God would give you the strength and wisdom to follow His commands. Ask Him to help you guard the women in your life by making you into a strong leader.

Women: Pray for the men in your life, that God would increase their desire to live for Him and help them walk in His design for protecting His creation.

4.2

SELFISH PASSIVITY

If you're a man, consider how you have struggled with this very issue. It's important for us to realize that passive men are deeply damaging to humanity's flourishing. We see this clearly at the Fall—Adam was the first passive man. First, Adam did not step up to lead his wife away from sin. Then, after sinning himself, he didn't man up and confess his brokenness, but instead shifted blame to his wife and even to God.

> When have you blamed God for your circumstances rather than taking responsibility for your own sinful actions?

In Genesis 12, God called Abram to leave his home and walk in a journey of obedience. Along the journey, Abram veered into the ditch of passivity.

> Read Genesis 12:10-20. How was Abram passive in this situation? Why do you think He reacted this way?

> What were the effects of Abram's passivity on his wife? Himself? Those around him?

> What might have changed had Abram chosen to lead, love, serve and protect what God had entrusted to his care?

Take a look at King David. While at times in Scripture he is a great example of a man who embraced godly manhood, in this story, he chose passivity.

Passivity starts with one compromise, which usually leads to others.
Read 2 Samuel 11:1. What was David's first compromise?

Passivity can take many forms. It can mean doing nothing, as we saw with Adam in the Garden. However, passivity can also mean giving your heart over to compromise and desire, rather than choosing self-control. Selfish passivity subtly works its way into every aspect of our lives. To continually walk in passivity as a man is to continually live in rejection of God's beautiful design.

List some things David gave his heart over to. Then, circle those you struggle with the most.

For Young Men: Are there any people you need to seek forgiveness from because of your passivity? If so, what steps will you take to make it right?

For Young Women: Are you holding any bitterness toward a man because of his passivity? Explain. What steps will you take to find healing?

PRAYER

Guys: Take time to repent from your passivity. Confess your sin to the people you've hurt. Commit to reject passivity and choose to step into the difficult space of leadership in your family and church.

Girls: Ask God to help you overcome any bitterness you may have toward a man because of his passivity. Pray that God will help you forgive him and encourage him to embrace selflessness and self-control.

4.3

SELFISH AGGRESSION

Think back to our study last week. We discovered that the masculine heart is hard-wired for action, danger and achievement. However, when not submitted to the glory of Christ and the mission of Christ, that wildness of men's hearts can cause worlds of pain and devastation. When man's propensity to fight gets out of balance, he becomes a bully, tyrant or dictator.

Let's review the meaning of *headship*. If you need help filling in the blanks, refer to page 32.

> Headship is the unique _____ of the man in the work of establishing _____ for human _____.

Because of the Fall, men are now bent toward living out the role of headship in sinful ways, instead of loving, serving and protecting. The selfless, compassionate love of Eden has been replaced by ungodly domineering.

For example, David's passivity spread throughout his life. His actions also negatively affected the lives of the people around him. When David realized that his sin with Bathsheba had consequences, he sought to correct the problem. However, instead of taking responsibility for his actions by choosing confession and repentance, he chose to act in selfish aggression.

> Read 2 Samuel 11:6-14. In what ways did David utilize his position and power to sinfully manipulate the situation?

The pattern of sinful aggression rose up in David's offspring—most notably in his son Amnon.

> Read 2 Samuel 13:1-2,12-14. Note how Amnon acted with selfish aggression.

How men relate to women should be driven by recognizing their intrinsic value as image bearers of God. Instead, selfish aggression causes men to devalue women into objects created to satisfy their desires. The result: sexual sins. Instead of serving, protecting and celebrating women, men often exploit them as nothing more than objects for their pleasure.

Let's look at another example.

> Read Genesis 4:7. Notice that Cain killed his brother out of selfish aggression. When offended or challenged, how do you typically react? How do men and women demonstrate anger in different ways?

> Now read Genesis 4:9. Notice Cain's sarcasm. Some types of sarcasm can be funny. But in other instances, sarcasm is simply passive aggression and criticism. When has your sarcasm hurt others?

There are other obvious cases of men's selfish aggression, such as bullying and abuse. If you are an offender in an abusive situation, God sees your actions and will always bring hidden sins into the open. Repent, and seek forgiveness and help. If you are a victim in an abusive situation, it is critical that you immediately notify and seek the counsel of your group leader or pastor, as well as local authorities.

PRAYER

Men: Conclude this week's Bible study by asking the Lord to reveal to you any ways that you are acting in selfish aggression. Repent of your actions and seek forgiveness from the people you have hurt.

Women: Pray that God will reveal to the men in your life ways that they are struggling with selfish aggression and give them the courage to turn from it.

MAN'S REDEMPTION

WELCOME TO YOUR GROUP EXPERIENCE FOR SESSION 5 OF *A BEAUTIFUL DESIGN*.

Take a few minutes to review what we discussed in the previous session.

Grade yourself, on a scale of 1 to 10 (10 being very good and 1 being very poorly), on how well you are doing at living out God's design for your life. Why did you grade yourself the way you did? What is hindering you from more faithfully living out God's design?

Have you made an effort to submit to God's design for your life since beginning this study? How so?

What areas of your life are most difficult for you to submit to God's good design? What is one step you could take this week to entrust that part of your life to the Lord?

Since God is Creator, that means He has the authority to determine the world's design and function. It is God's role as Creator to tell us, "This is how life works best." When we take matters into our own hands and say, "No, no, this is how it works best," we will find ourselves disappointed and frustrated. This isn't to say that if we submit to God's design, we will suddenly have a wonderful and fulfilling life; instead it means that to reject our infinite and wise God's design for life is foolish and dangerous. However, like Adam and Eve, we have rejected God's perfect design in favor of our own. When Adam and Eve did this, the results were devastating—they were cut off from God and each other. Thankfully, that is not the end of the story. In the moment they sinned, God promised to do something about their sin. Today, we will explore that remedy—how we, in our brokenness, might be redeemed so that we might embrace God's perfect design and purpose for us.

SMALL GROUP STUDY

DISCUSS THE STUDY USING THE QUESTIONS BELOW.

Share about a time when you felt helpless to fix a problem you were facing. Why did you feel that way? What did you learn from that experience?

Last week we talked about the effects of the Fall. When Adam and Eve rebelled, they invited sin and death into God's good world. That which was pure and good became broken and corrupt. Everything, including us, now possesses the stench of death. Sin has left us in a helpless state. If you are honest, you have felt this. There are certain things about the way you live and think that are not right but you just can't seem to change. Thankfully, the gospel is good news to the hopeless because it tells us about how God chose to step into our dark, broken world. He deliberately reached His holy, pure hands into the stench of death so that He might bring life.

READ EZEKIEL 37:1-11.

This vision was not just about Israel's national exile. It was also about a bigger spiritual exile that we all experience. In what sense were all of us *exiled* or *separated*, from God?

Why is it essential that we recognize we all were once separated from God? Why is such recognition important when it comes to how we understand manhood and womanhood?

This valley was the picture of death. Not only was it filled with bones, but they were dry bones—completely devoid of any kind of life. Even though we might not recognize it, the Bible tells us that we are all dead in our sin, separated from God. In other words, all of us are living in the valley of dry bones; the valley represents our separation. Our sin has corrupted our hearts so deeply that we have all refused to walk in God's design. Until we recognize this fact, the resurrection of Jesus and what He offers us because of it won't really mean much to us.

READ ROMANS 3:10-18 AND EPHESIANS 2:1-3.

What similarities do you see between these verses and Ezekiel's vision?

Why do you think Ezekiel responded the way he did to God's question (v. 3)? What does this tell us about the answer to our separation from God?

When Ezekiel saw the picture of death, he knew that the only way the bones could live was if God did something miraculous. No matter how much those bones might have wanted to live, they were powerless to change their condition. It's the same way with us. Only through God's mercy and grace can the separation between us be bridged.

> Why is it important that Ezekiel spoke the Word of God over the dry bones before they started to live?
>
> What is the Word that God uses to bring us to life (Eph. 2:4-8)?

The people of Israel felt like all was lost. They had seen their entire country burned to the ground before being exiled, they were deported out of their country and into another. Yet the promise from God to the dry bones was, "I'll put you back together, an exceedingly great army. I'll enter the chaos, enter the brokenness and bone by bone, sinew by sinew, muscle by muscle, flesh by flesh, I'll breathe life into you. And where you have been dead, where the stench of death has reigned, you will live. Then, the stench of death will change to the aroma of My presence."

READ ROMANS 6:1-11.

> What does it mean to "walk in a new way of life" (v. 4)? What unique temptations do young women and men face to return to their old selves?
>
> In what ways do you need Jesus to breathe new spiritual life into you? As a group, how might we help each other embrace Christ's work of spiritual transformation in our lives?

If you have trusted in Jesus, His resurrection tells you something very important about yourself—you are no longer a slave to sin. You have been brought from spiritual death to new life. You don't have to give into selfish aggression or passivity. Christ has given you a new identity as His child and empowered you with the Holy Spirit to begin glorifying Him by faithfully living out of His design for you as young women and men.

CLOSE IN PRAYER. COMPLETE PERSONAL STUDIES 5.1-5.3 BEFORE THE NEXT GROUP EXPERIENCE.

5.1

THE STENCH OF DEATH

As I write this on a dreary Saturday morning, our nation and the world mourn the loss of more innocent lives in another mass shooting. When thinking about such tragedies, we recognize that the created order is broken and in need of redemption. And our hearts feel it. The Fall has brought death in our world and its effects linger.

> Read Genesis 3:17-19. In what ways do you see the lingering effects of the Fall in this passage? How does death affect our lives as a result?

Read Ephesians 2:1-5. The apostle Paul is describing the life of the follower of Christ in two periods—*what you were* and *what you are now*.

> Read Ephesians 2:1. What was the word Paul used to describe what you were before knowing Christ?

> Before Christ, _____ (your name) was _____.

There is something in the masculine spirit that hates to fail. Men are wired with a desire to win. Even when it comes to their relationship with God, men try to prove their masculinity by being "man enough."

> Read Ephesians 2:8-9. If we are dead because of our sin, how are we made alive?

Maybe some of you feel insulted by the simplicity of that question. Maybe you're tempted to quickly write down a "Sunday school answer" and move on. But, don't miss the gravity of this doctrine. Here's what Arthur Pink says:

> Growth in grace is growth downward. It is the forming of a lower estimate of ourselves. It is a deepening realization of our nothingness.[1]

We cannot will ourselves to be better men (or women). Ironically, the very thing men do to try to prove their masculinity is actually what disqualifies them from being successful in imaging God through Biblical headship.

Review Ezekiel 37. Who was it that breathed life into the dry bones? Describe the scene this passage brings to mind.

If we are to find redemption from death and the stench of death, we will only find it when we recognize our complete and utter dependence on God to make us alive again.

How can you live in a way that displays the thankfulness and affection you have for your Savior?

PRAYER

If you're not a follower of Christ, consider taking time now to repent of your sins and confess Him as the Lord of our your life. Express to God your recognition of your dead status and your complete dependence on Him to be made alive. If you are already a follower of Christ. Express your unworthiness and thankfulness that God has made you alive.

5.2
MADE ALIVE

Let's get practical in our study today. Begin by reading 1 Corinthians 15:22.

Record the verse in your own words replacing "all" with your name.

What were some of the immediate ways that your life changed and "was made alive" when you trusted in Christ for salvation?

Where death has been present, the stench of death lingers. By God's grace, when we place our faith in Jesus Christ as Lord we are made alive again. And yet, the stench of our former status remains in areas of our lives. This is why Paul tells us that we must continually be conformed to the image of Christ (Rom. 8:29). There are parts of our lives that still do not resemble Christ.

For Young Men: What is one area of your life in which you still struggle with passivity? With aggression?

For Young Women: Make a list of how your relationship with Christ has changed your view of men. Are there any areas in which your view still needs to change?

As we engage with God's Word and confront sin in our hearts, the Holy Spirit removes that sin from us. Read Romans 8:1-11. What does Paul tell us is in opposition to the Spirit?

How should the actions of young Christian men toward women be different than those of worldly men?

The New Testament would call the parts of us that are yet to be conformed to the image of Christ, the *flesh*. Now, read verses 28-29.

Jot down the main idea of Romans 8:28-29 in your own words.

For Young Men: How does your new life in Christ impact the way you interact with women?

For Young Women: How can you help the men in your life find freedom from patterns of passivity or aggression?

Where you have been dead and the stench of death has reigned, through repentance and the life-changing power of the cross you will live and the stench of death will change to the aroma of God's presence.

PRAYER

I pray specifically for my brothers—that we would arise, wake up and let the light of Christ shine on us and that the glory of Christ would be seen. For those who've yet to follow Christ, I pray that you would give them the grace to completely submit their lives to you, God. And I pray for the boatload of us men today who continue to carry with us the stench of death. Might we be quick to confess, repent, get up and pursue again.

5.3

NO FAKERS

Don't "fakers" make you feel uncomfortable?

> Name some times when you have been fooled or seen people fooled by a "faker."

Although there's something in most of us that rises up when we encounter a fake, if we are totally honest, many of us are "faking it." However, many young men are not faking it to deceive, they're faking it to conceal. They are afraid to be true and honest. They are afraid if they let people in, then they'll be found out to be less than they portray themselves to be. So the fear of not measuring up drives the man's heart to pretend he's got it together.

> **For Guys:** How are young men tempted to "fake it"? Ask those who feel comfortable to share when they've been tempted to do so?

> **For Girls:** How are young women tempted to "fake it"? Ask those who feel comfortable to share when they've been tempted to do so?

Sometimes we even think we can fool God, that we can fake Him out with our right words and right actions. But God is not fooled.

> Read Hebrews 4:13. Summarize the verse in your own words.

God sees into the deepest part of your heart. He knows all your fears, flaws and failures. He knows that in your own power you're never going to live up to what He desires for you to be. You're never going to live up to what your family or friends need you to be. If that's the case, then what do you do?

Read Zechariah 4:6. What is the Lord's message in this verse?

We all must realize that it is only through the power of the Holy Spirit that we will be the men or women that God wants us to be. So guys, quit trying so hard to do this manhood thing in your own power. Understand this is not a call to be passive. We don't sit around on the couch until the Spirit shows up and moves us off it. Instead, we release control of our lives to the Lordship of Christ and allow the Spirit to strengthen us, guide us and empower us as we walk in this world as sons, brothers, men.

PRAYER

Guys: Take a moment and be totally honest with the Lord. Confess your attempts to fool God and conceal what's really going on in your heart. Submit yourself to Him and ask the Holy Spirit to empower you and lead you to be the man God desires for you to be.

Girls: Pray that the men you know will have the courage to be honest before God. Ask the Lord to give you wisdom on how to encourage them to totally trust in the Lord.

WOMAN'S PURPOSE

WELCOME TO YOUR GROUP EXPERIENCE FOR SESSION 6 OF A BEAUTIFUL DESIGN.

Take a few minutes to review what we discussed in the previous session.

While all women and men are sinners in desperate need of God's grace, their struggle with sin reveals itself differently. How so?

What unique struggles do you face as a young man?

What unique struggles do you face as a young woman?

Do you live with an active awareness of your desperate need for Jesus? Why or why not?

How aware are you of your daily need for Christ? How would a greater awareness help you grow in your walk with Christ?

Last week we saw how the created order has been broken by sin, including how we think about manhood and how we live as men. We also saw how Christ is the solution to our brokenness. This week will focus on God's design for women. While women and men are equal in dignity, value and worth, they are clearly different. As unique and valued people, God intends for women and men to reflect His image in equally important but different ways. Today, we will focus on God's purposes for women.

SMALL GROUP STUDY

DISCUSS THE STUDY USING THE QUESTIONS BELOW.

In a wedding ceremony, who gets more attention, the bride or the groom?

If we judged our understanding of women and men solely on observations of wedding ceremonies, what kinds of conclusions might we draw?

When attending a wedding ceremony, one of the first things we notice is that the bride takes center stage. Flower petals are placed on the floor for her, the music changes for her and everyone stands to honor her as she enters. If we got our understanding of men and women from weddings, we might assume that the wife is more important than the husband. Many people today make the opposite claim about the Bible's teaching on marriage, saying that it elevates men over women. Much like basing all you believe about women and men on weddings, this assumption doesn't hold up when we look closely at God's design for women and men in creation. Today we will see that while equal in dignity and value; God designed women and men to complement one another so that both might reflect His glory more clearly.

READ GENESIS 2:18-25.

Two things stand out in this passage that people today are likely to miss. First, in many ancient cultures, women were considered property and a man with lots of wives was considered wealthy and powerful. And yet, God created one woman for Adam. Secondly, we see that God intended for man to leave his family and start a new family with his wife. In Ancient Near Eastern culture, it would have been assumed that the woman would leave her family and be absorbed into her husband's. However, God intends for those who marry to start a new family that takes priority for both.

Look back over Genesis 1. What did God say about each thing that He created? What did God say was "not good" in Genesis 2:18? What does that tell us about His design?

While you may feel like marriage is a long way off for you, why is it important to think about God's design for marriage now?

Everything God made, He declared "good" (Gen. 1). In Genesis 2:18, however, something was declared "not good." A world without women or men, would not be good—God designed the two to complement each other and bring His good world to completion. While marriage may seem distant for you, thinking about God's design for marriage now will prepare you for the future and give you a deeper sense of how God would have you live out His design for your gender in the present.

> What does it mean to be a "helper fit for him" (v. 18)? Does this make women subordinate to men? Why or why not?

> What does it mean to be "one flesh" (v. 24)? What does that tell us about women and men and their roles in the marriage?

The word "flesh" in verse 23, literally means *person*. When a man and a woman marry, they become one person—they share everything. Everything one does affects the other. God designed husbands and wives to share all things and to serve each other as if they were one. The Hebrew word for "helper" (*ezer*) is used most often to describe God's role in the lives of His people, strengthening them to remain faithful to Him in difficult times (Ex. 18:4; Deut. 33:7; Ps. 33:20). It is not a subordinate role. In fact, the one who is being helped is often the weaker one, needing help in order to execute their primary responsibility. God made woman "a fit" for man. Women and men were created by God to complement one another, not compete against one another.

> Read Titus 2:1-5. What does this show us about God's design for women and their vital role in the church?

> How would you explain the unique role of women to someone who feels that the Bible discriminates against them?

Paul encouraged women to actively engage in the teaching ministry of the church by teaching other women and children. The word "homemaker" can also be translated *working from home*—this does not mean that women should not work outside the home. Again, the focus is on how God desires for women and men to complement one another. Women and men are vital to one another and to their God-given mission of making disciples.

CLOSE IN PRAYER. COMPLETE PERSONAL STUDIES 6.1-6.3 BEFORE THE NEXT GROUP EXPERIENCE.

6.1
BETTER TOGETHER

Merriam-Webster defines a woman as "an adult female person."[1] If you are a woman, live with one or know one, you might agree that this definition is sorely lacking when it comes to explaining all that a woman is. For sure, it doesn't come close to the biblical definition of a woman.

We know from Genesis 2 that God created both male and female, equal in value and distinct in purpose.

What are some ways women are similar to men? How are they different?

Why do you think God created man and woman similar and different?

Read Genesis 2:18-25. God said, "it was not _____" for Adam to be alone.

Everything thus far in Genesis had been weighed by God and given a positive assessment. Every portion of creation was evaluated as either good or very good. For the first time, we encounter something that is not good: man's lack of an equal companion.

What was special about Eve that made her fit to be Adam's partner?

As the Lord brought all the living creatures before Adam to name, Adam began to realize there was no one like him. The Scripture says in verse 20 that there was not a "helper" (ESV) or "complement" (HCSB) suitable for him. So, after already acknowledging Adam's need for a helper (v. 18), God fashioned the woman from one of Adam's ribs. He could have made her from the dust of the earth the same way He made Adam, instead He set the stage for the unmatched human intimacy found between a husband and wife by taking Eve out of Adam.

How does our culture view marriage? How does this compare to God's view of marriage?

As a student, why is it important to understand God's design for marriage? For women and men?

If our nation's divorce rate tells us anything, it tells us that the culture we live in does not have a high view of marriage. While marriage may not currently be on your radar, its important to begin cultivating a proper view of marriage now so that you will prepared to be a faithful, godly and committed wife or husband in the future.

Read 1 Corinthians 7:32-35. What are the spiritual advantages of singleness?

A woman who is not married is not less of a person just because she doesn't have a husband. God has created all women with value and they are complete in Him. In fact, singleness provides opportunities for women to serve the Lord in unique ways not available for a woman who's married. Married or single, God has strategically and purposefully created all women according to His beautiful design.

PRAYER

Take a moment to pray thanking God for creating women. Thank Him for creating us to live in community with one another. Pray that God would prepare you to be a faithful, committed spouse in the future.

6.2

A HELPER FIT FOR HIM

Having the resources to help someone in need and being able to extend that help is usually a satisfying feeling. We feel useful and valuable—like we have a part to play. In the same way, God gave woman a specific part to play in His beautiful design. He created her to be a helper.

Genesis 2:18 tells us that God wanted to make a helper fit for the man. God made a helper *like* Adam in the sense that she was human and *fit* for him because she would be the complement to help him rule and reign over the earth.

> Read Genesis 2:23. How did Adam respond to the creation of Eve?

He didn't say, "Oh great, someone else for me to take care of!" or "I wish you'd made her a blonde." Instead, there seemed to be a sense of relief in his words, "at last, bone of my bones and flesh of my flesh" (v. 23). He now had the counterpart he needed and desired.

In your small group experience this week, you learned that "helper" is actually the Hebrew word *ezer* and is most often used to describe the way God helps man. Being a helper is not inherently inferior. A helper is one who supports someone who holds the primary responsibility but cannot fulfill it on his own.

> Read Ephesians 5:22-23. What does it tell us wives should do? Why do you think people sometimes view this passage in a negative light?

Because of the Fall, both men and women can read this passage and interpret it in equally incorrect and negative ways. If we look back in Ephesians 5, we see that Paul was giving the church at Ephesus some guidelines for Christian living. In verse 21, he told them to be filled with the Spirit and to give thanks while "submitting to one another in the fear of Christ." After his command to submit to one another as Christians, he told wives to submit to their husbands. At the time Paul wrote this, it would have been typical for wives to be told to obey their husbands. It is significant that Paul used the Greek word *hypotasso* here, which translates "submit."[2] God has set an order. He gave men the job to love their wives as Christ loved the church and for women to submit to them as unto the Lord.

What can single people learn from this passage? How is Paul's picture of love and marriage different from the world's understanding?

For Young Men: What is the most challenging responsibility for husbands in Ephesians 5:25-28? How do you find enjoyment in God's unique design for you as a man?

For Young Women: How do you feel about the standards for wives in verses 22-23? How do you find enjoyment in God's unique design for you as a woman?

It's easy for women to think the standards set for them are too hard to live up to, especially when overlooking the role of the husband to love them as Christ loved the church. That is a weighty responsibility for men. The language in Ephesians 5 reminds us that men, with Jesus as their example, should not use their power to oppress but should give up themselves out of love. Neither role is easy, but when men and women live in these roles, it is a picture of the gospel.

PRAYER

Women: Pray for grace to be able to live out the purpose of *helper* God has given to you.

Men: Pray for grace to love the women in your life in a way that leads to their greatest flourishing.

6.3

LIVING IT OUT

Women, single or married, can live out their God-given purpose of being a helper in the home, the church and the workplace. We've already looked at Paul's commands to husbands and wives in Ephesians 5. The husband is to sacrificially love his wife, while the wife is to lovingly submit to her husband. He leads and she helps in his role of headship.

Let's look at another passage that speaks to the role of women.

> Read 1 Peter 3:1-2. Summarize it in your own words.

This passage reminds women that living in the role God gave them is a testimony to the Lord. God can use it to draw unbelievers to saving grace.

> Read Philippians 2:14. When have you been frustrated by or complained about doing something you know is the right thing?

> What is going on in our hearts when we do that?

We must remember that our words hold great power. We should use our words to build up and not to tear down.

> When have you observed a wife dishonoring or disrespecting her husband? Briefly describe the scenario in your own words.

> Read Proverbs 31:30. What kind of woman is to be praised? What are some practical ways you can strive to be this kind of person?

The Proverbs 31 woman, as she is commonly called, was praised by her husband and called blessed by her children. She had many great qualities and characteristics, but the one that stood above them all: She feared the Lord. This did not mean she made decisions out of fear, but had a reverence and awe of the Lord that caused her to trust Him regardless of circumstances. That kind of trust frees you to flourish. Remember, the partnership between men and women is not limited to marriage and home. Men and women need to work together to serve the church.

Read Acts 18:24-28. How did this husband/wife duo minister together?

Aquila and Priscilla were not only partners in life and in the home, but also in ministry. Other women in Scripture, such as Esther, Ruth and Mary, are lifted up as examples of faithful, kingdom-minded people. Jesus Himself elevated the value and place of women and showed that they had significance in his purpose and plan. Their significance did not change their role to headship or give them permission to usurp the authority and responsibility of a man. However, it did help us see how vital women are to the mission of God in the world.

Another note about women serving with men in the church: Ephesians 5 tells wives to submit to *their* husbands. They are not commanded to submit to all men, only to recognize man's God-given position of leadership and to come alongside as helpers to their future husbands. Women should cultivate and use their gifts within the body of Christ to further the gospel message.

PRAYER

Thank God for the unique opportunities He has given you as a young man or woman to serve Him. Pray that you would continue to embrace opportunities to grow in Christ and serve His church.

WOMAN'S HURDLES

WELCOME TO YOUR GROUP EXPERIENCE FOR SESSION 7 OF A BEAUTIFUL DESIGN.

Take a few minutes to review what we discussed in the previous session.

Last week we discovered that God created women to be helpmates to their husbands. What does it mean to be a helpmate?

Does that make women subordinate to men? Does it make their role lesser? Why or why not?

Girls, how should knowing that God created you to be a helpmate to your future husband shape the way you live in the present?

A helpmate is a person who helps someone with primary authority. Far from a lesser role, helpmates are often more capable than the one they help. The Hebrew word for helper is often used of God in the Old Testament (Ex. 18:4; Deut. 33:7; Ps. 33:20). This role reminds us that God created women and men to complement one another in their roles as His image bearers. God has given men and women the same purpose: to glorify Him (Isa. 43:7). However, God has tasked them with living out that purpose in different but complementary ways. While created for God's glory, it is important to note that women, like men, have fallen short of God's glory (Rom. 3:23). Today, we will explore some of the unique struggles women face this side of eternity.

SMALL GROUP STUDY

DISCUSS THE STUDY USING THE QUESTIONS BELOW.

In what ways do guys and girls struggle with sin differently?

Why are the struggles of young men and women different?

Women and men were both created in the image of God. Still, they are distinct from one another in several significant ways. This can be seen in how each struggles with sin, failing to reflect God in their own unique ways. Men are prone to selfish passivity and selfish aggression—husbands are tempted to abuse their God given headship over their wives through physical and emotional abuse rather than self-sacrificial love. Conversely, women are tempted to rebel against God's design through the disordered desires of comparison and perfectionism. Today, we will look to Christ to reorder our desires for His kingdom and glory.

READ GENESIS 3:13-16.

What consequences did Eve face for disobeying God (v. 16)? How do we see these consequences today?

How does Eve's punishment compare with Adam's (vv. 17-19)? How did their decision to sin affect the world and their day-to-day lives?

How did God say women's desires would be frustrated by their husbands (v. 16)? What does this tell us about the unique struggles women face?

The decision to disobey God changed everything for Adam and Eve. They went from living in a perfect world in perfect fellowship with God to living in a world deeply scarred by pain and death. For both Adam and Eve, their fall invited pain and frustration into their lives. Eve would experience pain through childbirth and Adam through difficult work. Both would experience frustration in their relationship. Because of the Fall, women would desire to hijack the God-given authority of their husbands and men would desire to abuse their authority by being aggressive and overbearing.

How do you see the curse at play even today? As young women and men, why is it important to be aware of the unique struggles each gender faces?

READ JAMES 1:14-15 AND JAMES 4:1-3.

What desires lie at the root of our sins? Why is this important to recognize?

We all have a tendency to think of sin solely in terms of outward behavior—lying, cheating, stealing and murdering—but James makes clear that sin begins in the heart. Because of the Fall, our desires are now disordered. Even our good desires are corrupt—we elevate good desires to ultimate status and these desires begin to enslave us, leading to further dysfunction.

What disordered desires do young men tend to give in to? What disordered desires are young women most prone to give in to?

Unlike men who tend to give into selfish passivity and selfish aggression, the disordered desires of young women often take different shape. They are more likely to struggle with comparison and perfectionism. Julia Oliphant, writing for *The Telegraph* said, "a recent study confirmed it. Women spend more time checking each other out than they do the opposite sex." Dr. Caroline Walters, a women's sexuality specialist, said women compare everything with each other, "from hairstyle to tan, shape, size, even body hair and fat distribution. Whatever we deem to be most important ourselves."[1] We check out in other women. Striving for such "perfection" is a sure path to frustration and neglects our identity and purpose as God's image bearers. We were not created to look and live better than other people, but to reflect God's glory and find joy in Him.

How can we identify and turn away from our disordered desires?

Read James 5:16. How might we help one another turn away from sin and set our hearts on Christ?

True growth requires repentance. It requires pulling up sin by its roots—our desires. We must ask God to help us see how our desires are out place and look to Christ to change the very things we long for. Ask yourself: *What do I want most in life? What would I be willing to sin to get? What would I be willing to sin to keep?* These questions will help you identify the misplaced desires that are keeping you from joy in Christ so that you can look to Him to change your heart.

CLOSE IN PRAYER. COMPLETE PERSONAL STUDIES 7.1-7.3 BEFORE THE NEXT GROUP EXPERIENCE.

7.1

DISORDERED DESIRES

We don't know much about Lot's wife. We just know she looked back and became a salty statue. But why did she look back? Was it out of curiosity? Longing for the past? Regardless of the reason, she disobeyed what the angels told her and paid the ultimate price.

Review the story of Lot in Genesis 19. You'll notice that he struggled to live out his biblical role of headship. Did his sin of passivity play into his wife's disobedience? Probably. Our sins always affect those around us. There is a good possibility that neither Lot nor his wife were living out the purpose for which God had designed them.

Read Genesis 19:30-36. Summarize the passage in your own words.

This could be the storyline of an episode of a day time talk show. "Lot, you are the father of not one, but both of your daughter's sons." The brokenness and dysfunction of this family is heartbreaking. The daughters felt helpless, so they took matters into their own hands. Their selfishly passive fiancés chose to ignore the warning of Sodom's doom, so they perished. The girls were left in a cave with their father, the man they believed was the only male left on earth. His leadership and care for his daughters was sorely lacking, evidenced by his willingness to offer them to an angry, lascivious mob of men in the hopes that the mob would disappear. Lot's daughters may have felt as though their survival and family heritage was dependent on them. So what did they do? They took control and tricked their father into sleeping with them.

Think of a time when you were desperate and took control of a situation. What was the outcome? What can you learn from this?

Many times the choices we make out of desperation soon cause regret, shame and heartbreak. Instead of looking to the Lord for help, we deem ourselves powerful enough to solve the situation on our own.

What are some ways you try to take control of situations rather than trusting God?

Read Genesis 3:6. Why did Eve eat the forbidden fruit?

God had given Adam and Eve the fruit of any tree in the garden, except this one. However, Eve agreed with the enemy that God must not have known best. The fruit was "delightful to look at" (v. 6) and she desired the wisdom it might give her. So she took it. It did not provide what it promised—sin never does. Adam, in his passivity, stood by and watched, then actually participated by eating the fruit as well. They were both left in the aftermath of shame and brokenness.

For Young Women: What are some ways men have become idols in your life?

For Young Men: When have you mistreated women? Take a moment to confess those times to God.

PRAYER

Meditate on James 1:14-15. Before you pray, take a few minutes to reflect on a time when your disordered desires led to sin. If you haven't confessed that to the Lord, do so now. Pray that His transforming power would invade your desires and make them like His.

7.2

COMPARISON

In a simple stroll down a mall concourse, we are bombarded with images of what women feel they should be. Athletic, young and sensual with seemingly flawless bodies. How do you measure up to that?

Comparison is the disordered desire for approval and validation. God wired the female heart to desire pursuit. When she feels pursued, a woman's heart leans in. Because of the fall, she is constantly wanting someone to look at her and say, "Yes, you are enough."

Right before the story of Lot being rescued from the destruction of Sodom and Gomorrah, we see the story of a woman, Sarai, who made poor decisions because she felt she wasn't enough.

In biblical times, a woman's worth, purpose and security were tied up in her ability to have children. By bearing a child, particularly a son, the family name would pass on and she would have someone to take care of her in her old age. If that pressure wasn't enough, Sarai had the added weight of God's promise that she and Abram would have a son. Yet, she remained barren.

> Read Genesis 16:1-4. How did Sarai try to fulfill God's promise to Abraham on her own?

> How did her insecurities lead her to make sinful decisions?

Time passed and Sarai remained barren. Her self-worth must have been shot. Her faith in God was wavering. She exchanged her trust in the Lord for her own attempt to be enough. Once her maid became pregnant with her husband's child, regret surely set in. Feelings of comparison and insecurity controlled her. Not only could she not provide what her husband wanted, someone else could and did and this was done with Sarai's urging. Sarai later did conceive and gave birth to the son God had promised, but it was after much unnecessary heartbreak. Sin crouches at the door of comparison, promising a feeling of security and worth but leaving its victim in a state of hopelessness and despair.

For Young Women: List some thoughts you have when you encounter a woman who seems to have it all together whether physically, emotionally or spiritually, what feelings does it bring up in you?

How do you usually respond to these thoughts?

For Young Men: When have you witnessed a woman you care about caught in the snare of comparison? Describe that situation.

Jot down one thing you can do this week to encourage the women in your life to live in their God-given security instead of comparing.

At the end of the day, comparison is competition. Women, don't make other females into rivals. Take opportunities to champion other women in their successes and encourage them in their failures.

PRAYER

As you conclude your study today, meditate on Psalm 139:14 and record a prayer to God below.

7.3
PERFECTIONISM

Women want to be noticed. They want to turn the heads and hearts of men. If a man, especially the man she loves, deems her worthy of pursuit she feels adequate. If she is not being pursued, she will assume it's because she is not enough. The consequences of the fall bring this hurdle of perfectionism.

Dr. Brene Brown, an author and professor at the University of Houston says, "Perfectionism is not the same thing as striving to be your best. ...Perfectionism is the belief that if we live perfect, look perfect and act perfectly, we can minimize or avoid the pain of blame, judgment and shame."[2]

In what areas of your life do you struggle with perfectionism?

How do you feel when the expectations you have for yourself don't line up with reality? Explain.

Are you a perfectionist? What do the following verses tell you about the pursuit of perfection?

Ecclesiastes 7:20

Galatians 3:3

Isaiah 64:6

Ephesians 2:8-10

We can never attain perfection. While we know that truth, we still fall into the perfection trap. Then when we come up short, we usually react in one of two ways: 1) We either give up in defeat and battle despair and depression or 2) we exhaust ourselves trying to control every waking moment of our lives in vain. Both responses are destructive to ourselves and others. And both paralyze us in the mission of glorifying God and making disciples. The enemy will take advantage of this low view or ourselves, piling on shame, guilt and accusations. Or he will tempt us to be prideful when others attempt to build us up with encouragement. Sometimes insecurity and pride are dangerously more similar than we realize.

For Young Women: In what areas of your life do you feel inadequate? What is one step you could take today toward finding your worth in who you are in Christ? Explain.

For Young Men: List two practical ways you can encourage the women in your life to fully trust God and not stumble over the hurdle of perfection.

Women in their disordered desires can create masks. These charades of having it all together often lead to even more discontentment and insecurity. As Brown says, perfectionism is "a twenty-ton shield that we lug around thinking it will protect us when, in fact, it's the thing that's really preventing us from flight." In the next session, we will talk about how to lay aside that weight and live in the freedom of the cross.

PRAYER

Take a moment and surrender to the Lord the areas of your life in which you are striving for perfection. Confess that because Christ is enough, you are enough. Ask Him to give you grace to walk in faith not trying to please men, but to please Him.

WOMAN'S REDEMPTION

A BEAUTIFUL DESIGN

WELCOME TO YOUR GROUP EXPERIENCE FOR SESSION 8 OF A BEAUTIFUL DESIGN.

Take a few minutes to review what we discussed in the previous session.

Last week we discussed some of the disordered desires women are prone to (comparison and perfectionism). In which of these areas do you most need to grow?

If you are a guy, why is it important that you understand the issues women tend to struggle with?

What desires lie at the root of the sins you struggle with (*Jas.* 4:1-3)?

Have you made efforts to uproot the desires that motivate the sin in your life? How so? If not, what is keeping you from doing so?

James could not be more clear—the reason we find ourselves fighting and quarreling with others is because of the selfish desires in our hearts. If we hope to overcome the various sins with which we struggle as young women and men, it is not enough to correct our wrong behavior. We need God to change our desires. We need Him to change our hearts. Today, we will see how God offers to do just that. God offers to redeem us, every part of us, including our manhood and womanhood. Today, we will focus on how God redeems womanhood in Christ.

SMALL GROUP STUDY

DISCUSS THE STUDY USING THE QUESTIONS BELOW.

Today, we will again look at how the power of the cross redeems. Our sinfulness is exchanged for His righteousness. In our brokenness, we can be whole.

> If you could change one thing that is broken in the world, what would you change? Why?

> Instead of turning to Christ, where do we often look for redemption? Do women turn to different things than men? Explain.

> How is comparing ourselves to Jesus different than comparing ourselves to others? Is there a sense in which comparison is for our good?

READ HEBREWS 12:1-2.

> Look back at Hebrews 11, particularly verses 32-40, who is the writer of Hebrews referring to as the "great cloud of witnesses" (12:1)? What can we learn from their example in terms of how we should live today?

> What weights or sins are currently hindering you from faithfully following Jesus? What would it look like for you lay these things aside?

> If we hope to overcome the sins that are hindering us, why is it crucial that we keep our eyes on Jesus (v. 2)?

The "weights" and "sins" in verse 1 refer to desires we discussed last week that drive our sinful behavior. If we hope to overcome these sinful desires, we must not look to ourselves. We are not awesome. We are not strong. If we want to get rid of the sinful attitudes that weigh us down and run this race with endurance, we must consider where our focus lies. What you're looking at matters. Jesus is the author and founder of our faith. You didn't find Jesus; He found you. When we take our eyes off ourselves and fix them on Jesus, there is new kind of humility, meekness and confidence because we know we can't, but He can.

> How can the writer of Hebrews speak of Jesus enduring the cross "for the joy that lay before Him" (v. 2)? How does Jesus' example encourage you?

READ ROMANS 8:1-4.

What does it mean to be "in Christ Jesus" (v. 2)? According to these verses, what has Christ accomplished for those who are in Him?

How should the reality of what Jesus has done for us make us humble? How should it also give us confidence?

If you'll take your eyes off of you and start to look at Him, there is this weird paradox that happens. There is an onset of humility now because we know we're not awesome, but there is this explosion of confidence because we know God loves us. And God doesn't love the future version of you any more than He loves the version of you right now. When Jesus died on the cross for our sins, He canceled out the debt we owed because of our sins. At the cross, you were purchased out of slavery into freedom through Christ.

For Young Men: How can you support and encourage spiritual growth in the women in your life?

For Young Women: How does your new life in Christ impact the way you interact with men?

Should the actions of a redeemed woman toward men be different than that of a worldly woman? In what ways?

CLOSE IN PRAYER. COMPLETE PERSONAL STUDIES 8.1-8.3 BEFORE THE NEXT GROUP EXPERIENCE.

8.1

RUNNING BUT GETTING NOWHERE

In the 1800s treadmills were used in English prisons to generate power for mills. Prisoners held onto a bar and climbed paddle blades for hours on end. Toward the end of the 19th century, treadmills ceased being used for production and were just used for punishment.

If you've ever used a treadmill for exercise, at times if can feel like punishment. Most people would choose an hour run through a park over thirty minutes on the treadmill. Even though the run is long and may include difficult terrain, at least you're going somewhere. With the treadmill, you're exerting lots of energy but going nowhere! This can be true of our spiritual lives, as well. We exhaust ourselves trying to reach a mark that we can not reach. We expend tons of energy only to find we've not gained any ground. This is why we need the gospel. It truly is good news!

In Matthew 23, Jesus spoke against the religious hypocrites. He told his followers not to follow the example of the Pharisees because they don't practice what they preach.

> Read verses 5-7. What was the motivation behind the Pharisees' actions? Explain.

> How does the Pharisees' desire to be admired relate to the woman's hurdles we discussed last week?

The Pharisees wanted to be noticed and admired. They sought recognition through their vain attempts at righteousness. Last week we learned that the two major hurdles women face because of the Fall are perfectionism and comparison, both of which are highly based on appearances. These hurdles aren't limited to the female race, however. Men also struggle in these areas.

If you keep reading in Matthew 23, Jesus goes to on say that the Pharisees will incur great misery and sorrow for their hypocrisy.

Read verses 25-27. What are the two illustrations Jesus used to expose their hypocrisy?

We would never eat our morning frosted flakes in last night's dinner bowl still caked with spaghetti sauce, even if it looked spotless on the outside. No matter how white you paint a tomb, it is still filled with deadness. Dirty dishes and white-washed tombs. Clean on the outside, but reeking of death on the inside. When we are reaching for righteousness through our own attempts, we too are like the Pharisees. We cannot simply look the part. It is futile to keep dressing up the outside, while the inside is rotten. It's like running on the treadmill, lots of action, but not going anywhere.

For an example of people who fell into the trap of perfectionism and comparison, read the story of Leah and Rachel in Genesis 29-30. How did each fall into the trap of comparison? How did each get out?

We all fall into the comparison trap at times. We don't see ourselves or our families the way we expected them to look so we fret, manipulate and work to try to change ourselves and others. Then, finally when we are stressed, exhausted and see no results, we turn to the Lord. The one who made us and knows every detail of us, is often our last resort.

PRAYER

Take a moment and read through Psalm 139. Offer these words as a prayer, thanking God for knowing you like no other. Pray that He would free you from the trap of comparing yourself with others and help you to live in the freedom of being His child.

8.2
FIXED POINT

If you've ever struggled with motion-sickness, you know it's no fun. Headaches, vomiting and an overall feeling of wretchedness are a few of the symptoms. Motion-sickness is caused when there is a miscommunication between your ears and eyes. Your inner-ear knows there is movement, but your eyes are focused inside the vehicle thus your brain gets mixed signals.

So what helps? One thing you can do is find a fixed point. If you are being tossed about in a boat, fix your eyes on the shoreline. If you are in a car, fix your eyes on the horizon or the road ahead of you. The key is not looking around inside the vehicle at the steering wheel or the dashboard, but something ahead of you, outside of your immediate environment. This aligns the signals sent to your brain and alleviates the symptoms felt.

We've established the fact that we all need redemption. Women in particular need freedom from the shackles that perfectionism and comparison create. But how? A fixed point. We need to take our eyes off ourselves and our current situation and fix our eyes on Jesus who is never-changing. Let's look at how this applies when it comes to the hurdles of perfectionism and comparison.

> Read Psalm 34:5 and record it in your own words.

Those who look to the Lord are radiant with joy. They may not be happy. Their circumstances may not have changed, but they have joy. Why? Because they are looking to the only One who can fulfill. The only One who can give security and worth. We can't be perfect. We can't measure up. We aren't enough. That's why we need a Savior.

> Read Romans 3:10-12. Who is righteous? Who seeks God? Who does good? Why is this important?

Second Corinthians 12:9 says, "But He said to me, 'My grace is sufficient for you, for power is perfected in weakness.' Therefore, I will most gladly boast all the more about my weaknesses, so that Christ's power may reside in me."

Sometimes, we can get so zoned in on the areas of our lives that aren't going as planned that we don't give God room to work through us. Our weaknesses take center stage and we become self-centered in our feelings of inadequacy. Paul reminded us that God's power is perfected when we are weak.

Jot down some of your weaknesses that you need to give over to God.

Now Read Romans 8:1-4. Why is there no condemnation for those in Christ?

God has done what we cannot do. We cannot obey the law, we cannot be perfect. Again, that's why Jesus came. The good news of the gospel is that we exchange our sinfulness for His righteousness. Through His blood, we are made new and we are not condemned.

For Men: How can you communicate the freedom of the gospel to the women in your life?

For Women: How will you apply the truth of the gospel to the way you think and live this week?

PRAYER

Take a few moments to examine your heart. Confess and repent of any strongholds. Ask Him to take your weaknesses and show His power through them. Share with a close friend this week what God is showing you and how they can keep you accountable.

8.3

THE GREAT EXCHANGE

This week, we've pressed in to realize our great need for grace. We can't be enough on our own. That's why we need Jesus—He is enough. While we can know and believe this is true, living it out can be a struggle. How can we fight sin and lay aside all that weighs us down so we can live out His purposes?

EXAMINE AND REPENT

No matter how long you've been a believer, there are areas of sin in your heart and life that need to be addressed. Examine your heart often. Ask for God to bring sinful attitudes, thoughts and actions to the light. Then repent, confessing and turning away from those sins.

Read Psalm 139:23-2. Summarize the main theme and model your own prayer after these words.

Sometimes, extremes are required in order to disrupt a sin cycle. It may mean changing routines, cutting off unhealthy relationships or taking other serious measures to quit a sinful habit. Don't take sin lightly.

What are some actions you might need to take in order to disrupt a sin cycle in your life?

In what ways are you sometimes tempted to take sin lightly? How can you guard against this in your life?

ACCOUNTABILITY

If you are struggling with a certain sinful action or attitude, don't fight it alone. We need community and accountability to live worthy of God's calling on our lives. Whom do you trust? Take a moment to jot down the names of those people. Make a point to confide in one of these people this week. Tell this person about your struggles and ask for their prayers and encouragement.

PRAY AND BELIEVE

Too many times, we fall into sin because we are trying to do life on our own. We only call on God if catastrophe strikes. This might not be our actual mindset, but it's what we practice. Instead, be intentional about your prayer life. Start each day praying for grace for the day. Pray for your eyes to see Him working and for strength to follow Him.

Read Romans 7:14-25. What did Paul admit about his actions? What does this say about the presence of sin in our lives?

Read and summarize each of the following verses:

Romans 8:1-2:

2 Corinthians 5:17:

Lamentations 3:22-26:

Isaiah 44:22:

Jeremiah 29:11-13:

God is who He says He is and we are who He says we are. When it's hard to believe, read the truth and ask for grace to believe. He will even help us in our unbelief! Remember that you are vulnerable to sin when you entertain Satan's lies. You can't defend yourself with the truth if you don't know the truth.

Read Isaiah 61:1-3. Note and highlight the exchanges that happen in this verse. Now, take a moment to thank God for His grace.

PRAYER

Take a few minutes to thank God for the great grace He has shown you. Thank Him for His precious Word and ask Him to help you hide it in your heart. Commit to walk in His ways and live according to His truth.

TOGETHER FOR THE GOSPEL

WELCOME TO YOUR GROUP EXPERIENCE FOR SESSION 8 OF A BEAUTIFUL DESIGN.

Take a few minutes to review what we discussed in the previous session.

Men and women were created in the image of God. By their very nature, they share a fundamental identity as equal participants in imaging God. They possess equal responsibility to spread the glory of God and are equal recipients of grace. Men and women have been created in distinct ways and entrusted with complementary purposes that come together in a beautiful way for the advance of the gospel.

As we begin today let's take a few minutes to process what we've discovered so far:

Has this series changed the way you think about manhood or womanhood? How so?

What concept or idea has affected you the most throughout this series?

What has been most challenging for you to embrace or apply?

When men take up their responsibility within the created order, the home, the church and culture flourish. The church is the place where men, women, singles and married couples rally around the gospel. It is the believer's union with Christ that binds us together and it is this union that defines our lives.

SMALL GROUP STUDY

DISCUSS THE STUDY USING THE QUESTIONS BELOW.

What are common barriers to men and women working together? In your school? In church?

What hurdles stand in our group's path to living and working together for the gospel?

READ EPHESIANS 5:15-21.

In what ways does our culture seek to distract students from that which is wise and good?

What are some examples of what it looks like to live as wise young people?

For Young Men: How do you need to apply wisdom to your approach to living as a man?

For Young Women: How do you need to apply wisdom to your approach to living as a woman?

True wisdom requires that we deal honestly with the reality around us. The truth about the world and time we live in is that it is "evil" (v. 15). Therefore, to live wisely in this world as young men and women means to take note of the ways that our culture is redefining what it means to be male and female. To live wisely means to reject these redefinitions, instead trusting that the Bible is our authority and that every command and implication in the Bible is meant to lead us to life and joy. We must take biblical manhood and womanhood seriously. We should embrace who God made us to be and encourage those around us to do the same. Our hope is that by encouraging each other to live out the roles God has given us as women and men, that we would point people to Christ.

READ JOHN 13:34-35 AND 1 TIMOTHY 5:1-2.

What is distinct about the love Christians are to have for one another?

How effective is your group/church at treating each other as family? How can you improve?

When we take Scripture's teaching seriously, we see that we must be deeply and visibly *for* each other. Young men should think deeply about what it looks like to be *for* the women in their lives. Young women should think deeply about what it looks like to be *for* the men in their lives. Christ calls us all to an others-centered life, in which we constantly seek to live in such a way that we point the people around us to Christ.

For Young Men: What does it look like to be *for* the women in your life?

For Young Women: What does it look like to be *for* the men in your life?

As we wrap up our study, let's review by taking a few minutes to discuss the purposes, hurdles and redemption of men and women.

What might men and women working together well look like at your church?

CLOSE IN PRAYER. ENCOURAGE YOUR GROUP MEMBERS TO COMPLETE THE JOURNAL PROMPTS THAT FOLLOW.

JOURNAL

DAY 1

Now that our study is complete, spend some time this week reflecting on what you learned and how you will put it to practice. Journal your response to the following questions.

For Guys: Before we began this study, what was your understanding of what it means to be a man?

For Girls: Before we began this study, what was your understanding of what it means to be a woman?

How is God's design different from the way most people think about gender today? Has your understanding of gender changed since we began this study? How so?

Read Genesis 2:18-25 and spend some time meditating on God's good design of women and men. How is God's design for each unique from the other? How are they similar?

What in your life is distracting you from submitting to God's design? Record a prayer below, confessing these things to God and asking Him to empower you to submit to His design and live for His glory.

JOURNAL
DAY 2

Now that our study is complete, spend some time this week reflecting on what you learned and how you will put it to practice. Journal your response to the following questions.

Has your attitude toward the opposite sex changed since we began our study on God's design for women and men? How so?

What hinders you as a young woman or young man from honoring other students of the opposite sex? How will you seek to overcome these barriers?

Read Ephesians 5:22-33 and spend some meditating on God's design for men and women. What do these verses teach you about marriage? What should you be doing now so that you can be this kind of spouse one day, if you choose to marry?

Spend some time praying that God would help you mature in your relationship with Christ as a young man or young woman. Record your prayer below.

JOURNAL

DAY 3

Now that our study is complete, spend some time this week reflecting on what you learned and how you will put it to practice. Journal your response to the following questions.

How has your thinking about gender changed since we began our study on God's design for women and men?

In what specific ways have you been challenged to put the Bible's teaching on manhood and womanhood into practice?

What actions can you take to treat the men and women in your life more like people created in the image of God?

After all you've learned over the course of this study, how can you better pray for the men and women in your life? Record a prayer below.

SOURCES

SESSION 1

1. Russel Goldman, "Here's a List of 58 Gender Options for Facebook Users," *ABC News*, February 13, 2014, http://abcnews.go.com/blogs/headlines/2014/02/heres-a-list-of-58-gender-options-for-facebook-users/.

2. Rhonda Byrne, *The Secret* (New York: Simon and Schuster, 2006), 183.

SESSION 2

1. C. S. Lewis, *Mere Christianity* (Harper Collins: New York, 1952), 69.

2. C. S. Lewis, *The Weight of Glory* (HarperOne: San Francisco, 2001), 46.

3. Stephen J. Cole, "Psalm 139: No Escape from God," *Bible.org*, accessed February 4, 2016, https://bible.org/seriespage/psalm-139-no-escape-god.

4. "General Federation of Women's Clubs," *unicefusa.org*, accessed February 4, 2016, https://www.unicefusa.org/supporters/organizations/nonprofits/partners/gfwc.

SESSION 3

1. "Fatherless Homes Now Proven Beyond Doubt Harmful to Children," *Fathersunite.org*, accessed February 8, 2016, www.fathersunite.org/statistics_on_fatherlessnes.html.

2. Polly House, "Want your church to grow? Then bring in the men," *Baptist Press*, 2003, http://www.bpnews.net/15630.

3. Eric Mason, *Manhood Restored* (Nashville: B & H, 2013), 45.

SESSION 4

1. Robin Marantz Henig, "What is it about 20-Somethings?" *The New York Times*, August 18, 2010, http://www.nytimes.com/2010/08/22/magazine/22Adulthood-t.html?pagewanted=all.

SESSION 5

1. Aurthur Pink, *Spiritual Growth* (Ada: Baker, 1996).

SESSION 6

1. "Woman," *Merriam-Webester.com*, [cited 8 February, 2016]. Available from the Internet: http://www.merriam-webster.com/dictionary/woman.

2. S. M. Baugh, *ESV Study Bible* (Crossway: Wheaton, 2008), 2271.

SESSION 7

1. Julia Oliphant, "Why do girls check out other girls?" *The Telegraph*, August 29, 2013, http://www.telegraph.co.uk/women/womens-life/10272172/Why-do-girls-check-out-other-girls.html.

2. Brene Brown, *The Gifts of Imperfection* (Center City: Hazelden, 2010), 56.